Happy Christmas 2012

from Nannie & Granda.

x x x x

MOLLY BAKES

50 RECIPES FOR
CUTE CAKES ON LOLLIPOP STICKS

SQUARE PEG

Published by Square Peg 2011

4 6 8 10 9 7 5

First published in Great Britain in 2011 by
Square Peg
Random House, 20 Vauxhall Bridge Road,
London SW1V 2SA

www.rbooks.co.uk

Addresses for companies within The Random House Group Limited can be found
at: www.randomhouse.co.uk/offices.htm

The Random House Group Limited Reg. No. 954009

A CIP catalogue record for this book is available from the British Library

ISBN 9780224095228

The Random House Group Limited supports The Forest Stewardship Council (FSC),
the leading international forest certification organisation. All our titles that are
printed on Greenpeace approved FSC certified paper carry the FSC logo. Our
paper procurement policy can be found at www.rbooks.co.uk/environment

Photography: Noel Murphy
Design: Friederike Huber
Prop Styling: Wei Tang

Printed and bound in Italy by Graphicom

This book is for the Mickeys and the Goodies

CONTENTS

INTRODUCTION

I am going to let you in on a little secret. I only learnt to bake 2 years ago. That's right, I had never baked a single cake before then.

Here's how it came about: I had been obsessed by cupcakes for a while so, one Sunday afternoon a couple of years ago, I asked my mother to teach me how to make them because she is a baking queen. That afternoon, some very simple vanilla cupcakes were baked and it all made perfect sense. From then on I was besotted with baking beautiful, fluffy cakes. A month later I lost my job, the day before my 29th birthday. I might well have cried but, secretly, I was not entirely unhappy about it. That night I went home and baked cupcakes for my birthday party. It took me until 1 o'clock in the morning just to bake and frost 30. But my friends loved them. Over the months that followed, the more I baked, the more I fell in love. That's when Molly Bakes was born.

Not long after setting up a stall for selling cupcakes in Brick Lane Market, in London's East End, I stumbled across something that would change my life for the second time: Cake Pops. I knew instantly that people would love these, and I was right. After a year of perfecting the Molly Bakes Cake Pop I was asked to write this book. And here it is – all the tricks for creating the perfect pop.

I hope my story and the recipes that follow show that you don't have to be a brilliant baker or even an experienced cake decorator to make these. All you need is a few simple ingredients, some lollipop sticks and a little imagination.

Enjoy popping! Molly Bakes x

Cake pops are made by combining crumbled cake sponge and frosting, then rolling into balls or other shapes and coating in candy or chocolate.

Once you have mastered the various steps for making cake pops, it opens up a whole new world of opportunities for sweet treats on a stick. All you need is a little patience and careful planning.

One of the many beauties of cake pops is they can be made in advance and the individual steps don't even need to be done on the same day. To make the perfect pop it's worth setting some time aside and preparing what you can ahead of time. Things such as rolling the cake pop mixture can be done up to 3 days before you decorate the pops. Just refrigerate and then bring it out when you feel like popping!

All the cake pop recipes in this book are based on making batches of 20 medium pops, or 10 large ones, depending on the nature of the design.

Once you get the hang of it, cake pops are very simple to make because every cake pop recipe follows the same basic steps:

- Bake a cake and allow to cool
- Make the frosting
- Thoroughly crumble the cake
- Combine the cake and frosting and refrigerate
- Roll mixture into balls and refrigerate
- Insert sticks into the balls
- Dip cake pops in candy
- Decorate
- Package and give as a gift or
- Eat!

This basic technique is used for all the styles in this book. Once you have mastered the simple cake ball, it's easy to create any shape you like, whether a square, rectangle, cone or oval.

EQUIPMENT

Other than lollipop sticks and candy melts, you don't need any fancy
equipment for making cake pops (and for the Chocolate Cake Balls on
page 45 you don't even need those). If you have one, an electric mixer
is an easy way of mixing the cake batter, but otherwise a hand whisk or
even a wooden spoon is fine. You can find all the tools and ingredients you
need in your local supermarket, in cake craft shops, and online. A list of
recommended stockists is included on page 146. Later on, you might want
to invest in more specialist tools such as different-shaped cutters, brushes
and moulds for creating elaborate shapes.

YOU WILL NEED

Cake baking tin
The shape of your cake tin doesn't matter – round or square, anything is fine since you'll be crumbling the cake anyway. A good size for these recipes is a 25cm round tin or a 20cm square one.

Large mixing bowl
For mixing the batter, then later for crumbling the cake sponge and mixing with frosting.

Microwave-safe mixing bowl/s
Plastic bowls are best as ceramic or glass can get too hot and burn your hands. Make sure the bowl is microwave-safe for melting candy or chocolate.

Tray
For placing the rolled cake balls on as and when they are ready for dipping and during refrigeration. Any type of tray can be used.

Elevated metal wire rack
For cooling the cake sponge and for resting dipped cake balls on as they set.

Baking paper
For lining trays and for placing under the wire rack to catch drips.

Clingfilm
For wrapping the cake pop mixture during refrigeration.

Candy melts
Candy melts (also known as confectioner's chocolate or candy wafers) are a vegetable-oil-based product with similar properties to white chocolate. You can melt, mould, dip, drizzle and pipe candy melts. They come pre-coloured in white, black, pink, red, blue, orange, yellow, green or brown and are widely available in all good cake craft shops. See page 136 for creating new colours too.

Vegetable oil
For adding to candy melts for a smooth consistency.

Plastic spatula

For scraping down the sides of the mixing bowl when mixing the cake batter and for stirring candy or chocolate.

Lollipop sticks

For inserting into the cake pops. You can get them from cake craft shops and some supermarkets.

Polystyrene block or florist's Oasis

Poke holes into this so the cake pops can stand upright while they dry. Polystyrene is easiest to use and you can buy it from most craft stores. You can also use florist's Oasis, but wrap it in clingfilm so it doesn't get over your hands and into the cake.

Cocktail sticks

Keep a supply of these on hand – they are useful when glueing decorations onto cake pops and for creating texture.

FLAVOURS

The tried and tested recipes in this book are easy and you don't need to be an expert baker to make them. You're going to crumble the cake anyway so it doesn't matter whether it's even!

Feel free to mix the sponge and frosting recipes as you wish, but I find that you get the best flavours when you match the cake and frosting, i.e. vanilla sponge with vanilla frosting, peanut butter sponge with peanut butter frosting, and so on. You'll get deeper flavours by doubling up.

If you can use only good-quality ingredients when making these recipes you'll really notice the difference in taste. I recommend creamy butter instead of margarine, free-range eggs, and vanilla extract instead of essence. You can also use nature friendly flour, unrefined sugar and Fairtrade organic cocoa powder (see page 146 for stockists).

VANILLA CAKE

This light and fluffy vanilla cake makes a delicious base for a simple cake pop. Combine with classic vanilla cream cheese frosting for a wonderful buttery flavour.

Makes enough for approx. 20 medium cake balls

120g unsalted butter, softened, plus more for greasing
150g caster sugar
1 tsp vanilla extract
2 eggs, at room temperature
180g self-raising flour, sifted
4 tbsp milk, at room temperature

Preheat the oven to 180°C/gas mark 4. Lightly grease and flour a 25cm round cake tin or a 20cm square cake tin. Cream the butter and sugar until it turns pale and fluffy. Mix the vanilla extract into the creamed butter and sugar. Add the eggs, one at a time, mixing well between each addition. Add half the flour and then half the milk and mix until fully combined. Repeat with the remaining flour and milk.

Pour the mixture into the prepared tin and bake for 35–45 minutes, or until a cocktail stick inserted into the centre of the cake comes out clean. Once baked, leave to cool in the tin for 20 minutes and then turn out onto a wire rack to finish cooling.

VANILLA CREAM CHEESE FROSTING

80g unsalted butter, softened
40g cream cheese, softened
200g icing sugar, sifted
1 tsp vanilla extract

Cream the butter and cream cheese together. Gradually add the sugar, then continue to cream until light and fluffy. Finally, mix in the vanilla. Refrigerate for 30 minutes before using.

CHOCOLATE CAKE

This is a wonderfully rich chocolate cake, which creates my favourite baking aroma. Combine with the chocolate frosting for an unbelievably fudge-like texture.

Makes enough for approx. 20 medium cake balls

55g cocoa powder
250ml boiling water
120g unsalted butter, softened, plus more for greasing
200g caster sugar
200g self-raising flour, plus more for the tin
1 tsp baking powder
¼ tsp bicarbonate of soda
¼ tsp salt
1 tsp vanilla extract
2 eggs, at room temperature

Put the cocoa into a jug, pour in the boiling water and stir until combined. Preheat the oven to 190°C/gas mark 5. Lightly grease and flour a 25cm round cake tin. Cream the butter and sugar until pale and fluffy. Sift together the flour, baking powder, bicarbonate of soda and salt. Mix the vanilla into the creamed butter and sugar. Add the eggs one at a time, mixing well. Pour in the dry ingredients and gently beat until combined. Fold in the cooled cocoa until the colour of the mixture is even. Pour into the tin and bake for 45–60 minutes, or until a cocktail stick inserted into the centre of the cake comes out clean. Once baked, leave to cool in the tin for 20 minutes and then turn out onto a wire rack to finish cooling.

CHOCOLATE FROSTING

120g unsalted butter, softened
200g icing sugar, sifted
100g chocolate, melted and cooled (see page 42 for how to melt chocolate)

Cream the butter. Gradually add the icing sugar and then add the chocolate. Continue to cream until light and fluffy. Refrigerate for 30 minutes before using.

RED VELVET CAKE

This traditional American cake flavour is perfect for Valentine's designs and is delicious combined with the vanilla cream cheese frosting on page 22.

Makes enough for approx. 20 medium cake balls

250g self-raising flour, plus more for the tin
¼ tsp salt
1 tbsp cocoa powder
4 tbsp red food colouring
120g unsalted butter, softened, plus more for greasing
250g caster sugar
2 eggs, at room temperature
240ml buttermilk
1 tsp vanilla extract
1 tsp cider vinegar
1 tsp bicarbonate of soda

Preheat the oven to 180°C/gas mark 4. Lightly grease and flour a 25cm round cake tin or a 20cm square cake tin.

Sift together the flour and salt and set aside. In a cup or small bowl, mix the cocoa powder and red food colouring into a smooth paste, then set aside.

Cream the butter and sugar together until pale and fluffy. Add the eggs, one at a time, mixing well between each addition. Scrape down the sides of the bowl, then add the cocoa powder mixture.

In a measuring cup, whisk the buttermilk with the vanilla extract.

Now add a third of the flour mixture to the creamed butter and sugar, followed by half the buttermilk and mix until combined. Add another third of flour and the remaining buttermilk. Finally, add the remaining flour mixture and mix until just combined.

Combine the vinegar and bicarbonate of soda in a small cup. Allow it to fizz and then quickly fold into the mixture. Pour into the prepared tin and bake for 30–45 minutes, or until a cocktail stick inserted into the centre of the cake comes out clean.

Once baked, leave to cool in the tin for 20 minutes and then turn out onto a wire rack to finish cooling.

PEANUT BUTTER CAKE

Kids will love this quirky cake recipe. Combine it with peanut butter frosting for a full-on flavour or go for the classic chocolate frosting on page 25.

Makes enough for approx. 20 medium cake balls

180g self-raising flour, plus more for the tin
1 tsp baking powder
80g unsalted butter, softened, plus more for greasing
50g smooth peanut butter
150g caster sugar
2 eggs, at room temperature
125ml milk

Preheat the oven to 180°C/gas mark 4. Lightly grease and flour a 25cm round cake tin or a 20cm square cake tin.

Sift together the flour and baking powder and set aside.

Cream the butter and peanut butter until combined. Add the sugar and continue to cream until pale and fluffy. Add the eggs, one at a time, mixing well between each addition. Add half the flour, followed by half the milk and mix until combined. Repeat with the remaining flour and milk. Pour the mixture into the prepared tin and bake for 35–45 minutes, or until a cocktail stick inserted into the centre of the cake comes out clean.

Once baked, leave to cool in the tin for 20 minutes and then turn out onto a wire rack to finish cooling.

PEANUT BUTTER FROSTING

80g unsalted butter, softened
40g smooth peanut butter

200g icing sugar
1 tbsp milk

Cream the butter and peanut butter together. Gradually add the sugar, then continue to cream until light and fluffy. Finally, mix in the milk. Refrigerate for 30 minutes before using.

TOFFEE CAKE

Give your cake pops a traditional English twist with this mouthwatering toffee flavour. Combine it with toffee frosting and evoke childhood memories.

Makes enough for approx. 20 medium cake balls

200g self-raising flour, plus more for the tin
1 tsp baking powder
150g unsalted butter, softened, plus more for greasing
150g light muscovado sugar
2 eggs, at room temperature
1 tsp vanilla extract
160ml milk

Preheat the oven to 180°C/gas mark 4. Lightly grease and flour a 25cm round cake tin or a 20cm square cake tin.

Sift the flour with the baking powder and set aside. Cream the butter and sugar together until pale and fluffy. Add the eggs, one at a time, mixing well between each addition. Mix in the vanilla extract. Add half the dry ingredients and then half the milk. Add the remaining dry ingredients, followed by the rest of the milk, and mix until combined. Pour the mixture into the prepared tin and bake for 35–40 minutes or until a cocktail stick inserted into the centre comes out clean. Once baked, leave to cool in the tin for 20 minutes and then turn out onto a wire rack to finish cooling.

TOFFEE FROSTING

60g unsalted butter, at room temperature
60g dulce de leche
200g icing sugar

Cream the butter and dulce de leche together until well combined. Gradually add the icing sugar and mix until smooth. Refrigerate for 30 minutes before using.

LEMON CAKE

My much-loved lemon cake recipe is a favourite in the spring. Combine it with zesty lemon frosting and try it with the Easter Bunnies.

Makes enough for approx. 20 medium cake balls

200g self-raising flour, plus more for the tin
1 tsp baking powder
¼ tsp bicarbonate of soda
½ tsp salt
120g unsalted butter, softened, plus more for greasing
200g caster sugar
Zest of 1 lemon
2 eggs, at room temperature
125ml full-fat yoghurt

Preheat the oven to 180°C/gas mark 4. Lightly grease and flour a 25cm round cake tin or a 20cm square cake tin.

Sift together the flour, baking powder, bicarbonate of soda and salt. Set aside.

Cream the butter and sugar until pale and fluffy. Mix in the lemon zest, then add the eggs, one at a time, mixing well between each addition. Now add the dry ingredients in 1 batch and mix until just combined. Fold in the yoghurt.

Pour the mixture into the prepared tin and bake for 35–45 minutes, or until a cocktail stick inserted into the centre of the cake comes out clean.

Once baked, leave to cool in the tin for 20 minutes and then turn out onto a wire rack to finish cooling.

LEMON FROSTING

120g unsalted butter, softened
200g icing sugar

Zest of 1 lemon
1 tbsp milk

Cream the butter until very soft. Gradually add the sugar and then continue to cream the mixture until it is light and fluffy. Mix in the zest and finally the milk. Refrigerate for 30 minutes before using.

METHOD

Once you have baked your cake and made your frosting, follow these steps to make your cake pop mixture, to shape the cake balls, and to coat them. A great trick is that you don't have to do all of this on the same day. The mixture stores well, so you can prepare it in advance and make your cake pop designs another day.

COMBINE THE CAKE SPONGE WITH THE FROSTING

Once you have the baked cake and frosting ready you can proceed to the next step of the cake pop process.

Crumble your cake thoroughly in a large mixing bowl. I normally do this by hand as it gives a finer crumb, but you can also use your food processor. You may want to remove the crusts of the cake with a sharp kitchen knife first to avoid any lumps.

Once you have crumbled the cake as finely as possible, take your frosting, a heaped tablespoon at a time, and begin mixing it in with the crumbs. You may not require all of the frosting, depending on how moist your cake is, so just use a little at a time. Keep mixing until you have a fudge-like texture. To see if it's ready, squeeze a little of the mixture in your palm – it shouldn't crumble and it should be pliable. If you add too much frosting your mixture will be soggy, sticky and heavy and the cake pops will just fall off the stick when you try to dip them.

Wrap the mixture in clingfilm and chill for at least 1 hour. When the mixture is firm but not too hard, it's ready to work with.

ROLL THE CAKE BALLS

Break off a small piece of the mixture, about the size of a ping-pong ball, and roll into a ball with your palms. It doesn't have to be perfect.

Place each ball on a tray lined with baking paper. Refrigerate for 15–20 minutes, or until they are firm.

You can either go straight on and just dip them as they are, to make simple cake balls, or shape them into a more adventurous design. In the Techniques chapter on page 132 I explain how to roll other shapes.

PREPARE THE CANDY MELTS

When using candy melts, it's important to make sure that all of your equipment, such as bowls and spatulas, is completely dry.

To melt the candy, you will need:

400g (1 bag) candy melts
Vegetable oil
Microwave-safe bowl
Plastic spatula

Place the candy melts in a microwave-safe bowl and heat in the microwave on medium power for 1 minute. Take out the candy melts and stir thoroughly. They may have just started to melt. Place back in the microwave and melt for a further 30 seconds. Stir again, making sure you scrape the bottom and sides of the bowl. Return to the microwave for a further 30 seconds, then give a final stir.

Melted candy doesn't normally achieve the same silky, runny consistency of melted chocolate. To make it easier to work with, you can add 1–2 tablespoons of vegetable oil per 400g bag of candy melts. Work enough oil into the candy with your spatula to create a silky consistency.

Candy will stay melted for about 20–30 minutes. If you stir your candy at regular intervals while working, it should keep from hardening. See page 137 for tips such as reheating candy melts.

INSERT LOLLIPOP STICKS

Take a lollipop stick and dip one end about 2cm deep into the melted candy. Immediately insert the stick into the top centre of each cake ball, about halfway through. Don't insert it too deep or too shallow. Place on a tray lined with baking paper to set. It should take between 1 and 2 minutes for the candy to set.

DIP THE CAKE POPS

Before you start it's best to pierce the holes into the polystyrene block which will hold the cake pops. This will save time and prevent accidents. Simply use a lollipop stick to pierce holes about 5cm apart.

To dip cake pops make sure the bowl is deep and quite full with candy so you don't need to tilt it. Hold an undipped cake pop by the stick and dip fully into the candy. When dipping, be sure to cover right to the top of the stick to secure the pop in place.

Gently tap the cake pop over the bowl to remove any excess candy. Place securely in the polystyrene block and allow to dry. Candy should take only 1–2 minutes to set.

DECORATE THE CAKE POPS

You can decorate with sprinkles or sugar decorations before the candy has set or leave the cake pops to dry completely if you're making one of the other, more elaborate designs in the book.

To decorate with sprinkles, simply take a teaspoonful of sprinkles and scatter them over the cake pop with a soft shake of your wrist. To decorate with sugar decorations, just press the decoration in the position of your choice, then place the pop in the polystyrene block to set.

See Techniques on page 132 for further tips on making sugarpaste decorations and on using cocoa butter for painting the cake pops. There you'll also find details of other equipment and ingredients you might need when tackling the more adventurous cake pop designs in this book.

DESIGNS

Start off with simple round cake pops and from there the pop world is your oyster. Why not try Lovehearts for Valentine's Day, Teddies for a baby shower, Ice Cream Cone Pops for a sunny day or Tricolour Pops just because.

SIMPLE POPS

Chocolate is a simple and easy-to-find alternative to candy melts for making cake pops. Try them with white, milk or dark to intensify the flavours. Decorate with nuts, candied orange, crystallised rose petals or drizzle with chocolate for a sophisticated gourmet pop!

Try these as cake pops or upside-down pops.

Makes 20 pops

Ingredients
20 medium cake balls, chilled
400g good-quality chocolate (white, milk or dark)
Decorations of your choice

Break up the chocolate into small pieces and place in a microwave-safe bowl. Heat in the microwave for 1 minute on the medium setting. Stir and repeat until chocolate has melted.

Dip the end of each lollipop stick 2cm deep into the chocolate and insert about halfway into the centre of each cake ball. Allow to set. Dip each cake pop into the melted chocolate, making sure the entire cake is coated, then remove and gently shake off any excess into the bowl. Decorate with sprinkles, nuts or confections of your choice. You can either insert into a polystyrene block or place face down onto baking paper to make upside-down pops. They will take 5 minutes to dry.

CAKE BALLS

What's brilliant about Cake Balls is you can make them with just what's in your kitchen cupboard. All you need is chocolate to coat them. So, if you don't have time to visit your local sugarcraft shop to find lollipop sticks, here's your solution – simple but oh so good.

Makes 20

Ingredients
20 medium cake balls, chilled
400g good-quality chocolate (white, milk or dark)
Decorations of your choice

Break up the chocolate into small pieces and place in a microwave-safe bowl. Heat for 1 minute on the medium setting. Stir and repeat until chocolate has melted.
   Place a sheet of baking paper under a wire rack. Dip the cake balls into the melted chocolate, using a cocktail stick. Make sure the entire cake ball gets coated in chocolate. Leaving the cocktail sticks in the balls, gently shake off any excess chocolate into the bowl. Decorate with sprinkles, nuts or confections of choice. Run the cocktail sticks through wire rack and leave to set for at least 5 minutes. Once the chocolate has set, remove the cocktail sticks.

LOVEHEARTS

Inspired by the sweets of the same name, these cake pops can be personalised for any occasion.

Makes 20 pops

Ingredients
20 medium cake balls, chilled
400g (1 bag) candy melts in base colour of your choice
100g (¼ bag) red candy melts

Equipment
5cm round biscuit or pastry cutter
Piping bag

For each cake ball, flatten and shape it into a 2cm-thick circle by pushing it into the biscuit cutter. Remove and smooth the edges with moistened fingers. Place in the fridge for 10 minutes to harden.

Melt the candy melts in the base colour. Dip each lollipop stick 2cm deep into the melted candy and insert a stick through the centre of each cake pop. Leave for 1–2 minutes until the candy has set.

Now dip each cake pop fully into the melted candy, making sure they get coated evenly. Remember to gently shake off any excess candy into the bowl, then place in a polystyrene block to dry.

Melt the red candy melts, then quickly pour into the piping bag so the candy doesn't set. Cut a small piece off the tip of the bag. Place a cake pop on a flat surface. Pipe the outline of a heart shape on the pop and then pipe Lovehearts messages. Repeat with the remaining pops.

TRICOLOUR POPS

Simple but very effective. Try this with contrasting colours of candy or varying shades of one colour.

Makes 20 pops

Ingredients
20 medium cake balls, chilled
400g (1 bag) candy melts in base colour of your choice
200g (½ bag) candy melts in a second colour
200g (½ bag) candy melts in a third colour

Melt the base colour of candy. Dip the end of each lollipop stick 2cm deep into the candy and insert a stick about halfway into the centre of each cake ball. Leave to set.

Now dip each cake ball into the base colour of candy, remembering to gently tap the excess into the bowl. Insert into a polystyrene block to dry. Drying time should be between 1 and 2 minutes.

Melt the second and third colours of candy separately. Now dip the top two-thirds of each cake pop into a contrasting or lighter/darker colour of candy. Make sure you dip straight down, to create even lines. Gently tap the excess into the bowl and insert into the polystyrene block to dry.

Finally, dip the top third of each cake pop into the third colour of candy. Gently tap off the excess and insert into the polystyrene block to dry.

If you want to take it further, why not try creating rainbows or flags with the different colours of candy.

MARBLE POPS

Marbling is another simple technique that will brighten up a basic round cake pop. You can start off with 2 colours and add as many as you like for total marble madness.

Makes 20 pops

Ingredients
20 medium cake balls, chilled
400g (1 bag) candy melts in base colour of your choice
100g (¼ bag) candy melts in secondary colour of your choice

Melt the base colour of candy. Dip the end of each lollipop stick 2cm deep into the melted candy and insert a stick about halfway into the centre of each cake ball. Leave to set.

Melt the secondary colour of candy and, using a tablespoon, add a little of the secondary colour to the bowl containing the base colour. Then use a cocktail stick to create swirls in the candy, taking care not to overmix the colours.

Slowly dip each cake ball fully into the melted candy and, as you dip, twirl it in the candy so that the colours swirl. This will create a gorgeous marble effect. Gently tap the excess candy into the bowl and insert the pop into a polystyrene block to dry.

Once you have mastered 1 extra colour, you can try experimenting with 2 secondary colours.

CLOUDS

Clouds are light and fluffy – just like cake – so one day I thought why not turn cake into clouds? Eureka!

Makes 10 pops

Ingredients
10 medium cake balls, chilled
400g (1 bag) white candy melts

Break up each cake ball and roll into 17 small, different-sized balls. Keep these small balls together in sets.

Melt the white candy. For each cloud, stick 7 balls together in a flat, horizontal cluster, using the candy as glue. Then make a separate cluster of 5 balls and stick it on the top of the first 7. Make a third cluster of 3 balls and glue it on top of the 5-ball cluster. Finally, stick the last 2 remaining balls on the topmost layer, again using the candy as glue. Leave on a tray lined with baking paper to set.

Dip the end of each lollipop stick 2cm deep into the candy and, taking extra care, insert a stick into each cloud. Leave to set.

Now dip each pop fully into the candy and gently tap off any excess. Insert into a polystyrene block to dry.

LIGHTNING

The weather forecasters might often get it wrong but these bolts are simple to make and you can be sure they'll always taste great.

Makes 20 pops

Ingredients
20 medium cake balls, chilled
400g (1 bag) yellow candy melts

Split each cake ball in half and shape each half into a triangular wedge about 2cm thick. Keep the wedges in pairs. For each pair, square off the pointed edge of one of the wedges with a knife and elongate the pointed edge of the second wedge.

Melt the yellow candy. Place a pair of wedges side by side, with the squared-off wedge on the left and the longer wedge about two-thirds of the way down on the right so you have something resembling a lightning bolt. Keep them in this position as you stick them together, using a dab of candy on a cocktail stick to secure them. Repeat for each pair of wedges.

One by one, dip the end of each lollipop stick 2cm deep into the candy, then take hold of a lightning bolt diagonally and insert the stick through the centre. Leave to set.

Dip each pop fully into the candy and shake off the excess. Insert into a polystyrene block to dry.

PRESENTS

Everyone loves giving and receiving presents. Make these extra-pretty by adding bows and polka dot patterns.

Makes 20

Ingredients
20 medium cake balls, chilled
100g (¼ bag) each pink, yellow,
  blue and green candy melts
50g white sugarpaste, kneaded
Edible glue
1 bottle white cocoa butter

Equipment
Rolling pin
2 paintbrushes (1 thin, 1 medium)
Artist's palette

Make bows in advance: roll out three-quarters of the sugarpaste to 2mm thick. Using a kitchen or small palette knife, cut it into 20 strips about 4cm long and 1cm wide. Fold the ends of each strip so they meet in the middle to form a bow, and apply some edible glue with a paintbrush to stick them in place. Now roll out the remaining sugarpaste to 2mm thick and cut into 20 strips, each about 2cm long and 7mm wide. Wrap a strip around the centre of each bow and glue into place. Place on a tray lined with baking paper and leave to set overnight.

Using your hands, shape half the cake balls into squares and the other half into rectangles. Leave to chill for 10 minutes.
  Place a sheet of baking paper under a wire rack. Melt the different colours of candy separately. Insert a cocktail stick into each square. Working with 5 squares per colour, dip each fully into the candy and shake off the excess. Place a bow on top of each one as you go and run the cocktail sticks through the wire rack. Leave to set.
  Melt the cocoa butter and pour 1 teaspoonful into the palette. Paint a vertical white ribbon down the centre of each side of the cake.
  One by one, take hold of each square by its cocktail stick and paint dots, swirls, stars and other patterns on it. Remove the sticks, then put them on a tray lined with baking paper and place in the fridge until the cocoa butter has set.

BAUBLES

Baubles are beautiful **party** decorations for any time of year. Make them sparkle with a little edible lustre spray.

Makes 20 pops

Ingredients
20 medium cake balls, chilled
100g (¼ bag) each green, blue, pink and yellow candy melts
40g white sugarpaste, kneaded
1 can edible silver lustre spray

Equipment
4 disposable piping bags

Make tops of baubles in advance: split the sugarpaste into 20 pieces and roll into balls with your hands. Flatten the balls slightly and make a hole through the middle of each one using the end of a lollipop stick. Leave to harden for a few hours. Once hardened, spray with the silver lustre spray. Leave to set overnight.

Melt each colour of candy separately. Working with 5 cake balls per colour, dip the end of each lollipop stick 2cm deep into the candy and insert a stick into each cake ball. Leave to set.

Dip each cake ball fully into the candy, shake off any excess and, while the candy is still wet, slide a bauble top down over the stick. Make sure the bauble top sticks firmly to the candy on the ball. Place on a sheet of baking paper with the stick facing up.

Working with 1 colour of candy at a time, pour each colour into a separate piping bag. Cut a small piece off the tip of each bag and pipe designs onto the cake pops.

Once the candy has set, spray the cake pops lightly with the silver lustre spray.

FAT BIRD POPS

Tweet tweet! These birds were loosely inspired by a certain social networking website.

Makes 20 pops

Ingredients
20 medium cake balls, chilled
200g (½ bag) each yellow and orange candy melts
Small edible heart sprinkles, for the beaks
1 bottle white cocoa butter
1 tube brown or black edible dusting powder

Equipment
Thin paintbrush
Artist's palette

For each cake ball, break off a 6g piece and split it in half. Shape each half into an elongated teardrop and then curve into a wing shape. Use the rest of the cake ball for the bird's body and elongate the back to form the tail.

Melt the 2 colours of candy separately. Dab a little candy on each wing with a cocktail stick and secure in place on the bird's body, pointed side up. Leave to set.

Working with 10 pops per colour, dip the end of each lollipop stick 2cm deep into the candy and insert a stick into each cake pop. Leave to set.

Now dip each pop fully into its respective candy colour. Insert into a polystyrene block to dry.

Using 2 heart sprinkles per cake pop, dip the curved end of each heart into the candy. Attach to the front of each pop to make the beaks.

Melt the cocoa butter and tint 1 teaspoonful with the dusting powder. Paint dots for the eyes. If you like, you can use other colours to paint patterns on the wings.

TROPICAL FISH

What could be more colourful than these tropical fish? Try painting stripes, dots and even scales. Spray with edible lustre for an iridescent look.

Makes 20 pops

Ingredients
20 medium cake balls, chilled
100g (¼ bag) each pink, green, yellow and orange candy melts
1 bottle white cocoa butter
1 tube each black, purple and blue edible dusting powder
1 can edible pearl lustre spray (optional)

Equipment
2 paintbrushes (1 thin, 1 medium)
Artist's palette

Break off a 6g piece from each cake ball and set aside. Form the larger ball into a large heart shape for the body. Shape the pointed end of the heart into a bulb for the mouth. Pinch and elongate the top curved edge to make the fin. Make sure the bottom of the fish is wide enough to push a stick into. Now take the reserved small balls and shape each one into a 'V', then curve each side outwards to form the tail.

Melt the 4 colours of candy separately. Working with 5 cake pops per colour, use a little candy to secure the tails to the back of the pops. Leave to set.

Dip the end of each lollipop stick 2cm deep into the candy and insert a stick halfway through the bottom of each fish. Leave to set. Then dip each pop fully into the candy and shake off the excess. Insert into a polystyrene block to dry.

Melt the cocoa butter. In the palette, tint 1 teaspoonful each with the 3 dusting powders and leave 1 teaspoonful white. Use the white colour to paint large dots for the fish eyes. Leave to dry and then paint a smaller dot inside the eye with the black colour. Use the purple and blue colours to paint tropical accents, stripes and dots on the pops. Insert into the polystyrene block and place in the fridge until the cocoa butter has set.

When set, spray each pop with pearl lustre if you wish, then place back in the polystyrene block to dry.

LIPS

Pucker up! Lip pops provide much fun. Make them as a set with the moustaches – they are a great gift for a newlywed couple.

Makes 20 pops

Ingredients
20 medium cake balls, chilled
200g (½ bag) each red and pink candy melts

For each pair of lips, mould each cake ball into the shape of an eye. Using a lollipop stick, make a slight indentation in the topmost curve of the 'eye'. Next, make an indentation running horizontally along the front. Finally, pinch the corners of the 'eye' and shape each corner upwards so you end up with something resembling a pair of lips.

Melt the 2 colours of candy separately. Working with 10 pops per colour, dip the end of each lollipop stick 2cm deep into the candy and insert a stick into each pair of lips. Leave to set. Dip each pop fully into its respective colour of candy and gently shake off any excess. Insert into a polystyrene block to dry.

MOUSTACHES

A pop that's fit for a true gent. Who said cake pops were just for the ladies?

Makes 20 pops

Ingredients
20 medium cake balls, chilled
400g (1 bag) black candy melts

Roll each cake ball into a log shape with your hands. Use a lollipop stick to make an indentation in the top centre and bottom centre of each 'log'. Squeeze and pinch the centre of the 'log' to shape the middle of the moustache. Now squeeze and pinch the ends, curling each one upwards to create a handlebar moustache shape.

Melt the candy. Dip the end of each lollipop stick 2cm into the candy and insert a stick into the centre of each moustache. Leave to set. Dip each pop into the candy, dipping from left to right to get an even coating. Insert into a polystyrene block to dry.

VINTAGE BUTTONS

I love all things vintage and these buttons remind me of Parisian flea markets. These cake pops have become the signature look of Molly Bakes. You can use silicone moulds to make the buttons or get creative and make your own shapes.

Makes 20 pops

Ingredients
20 medium cake balls, chilled
100g (¼ bag) each pink, yellow, lavender and green candy melts
50g sugarpaste
Food colouring paste
Edible sprinkles of your choice

Equipment
1 or 2 vintage button mould/s

Prepare the sugarpaste buttons in advance: take the sugarpaste, colour it with the food colouring paste and knead it. Push a piece into each hole in the mould/s, cutting off any excess with a small knife. Leave to dry on baking paper. Cover with clingfilm and store in a cool, dry place until ready to use.

When ready to make the pops, melt each colour of candy melts separately. Dip 5 lollipop sticks 2cm deep into the pink candy and insert halfway into the centre of 5 cake balls. Repeat, using 5 sticks per candy colour.

One by one, dip the cake pops fully into the different colours of candy, so you end up with 5 pink, 5 yellow, 5 lavender and 5 green pops, and decorate with the buttons. Sprinkle with coloured confetti sugar or hundreds and thousands.

Insert the pops into a polystyrene block to dry.

HANDBAGS

Treat yourself and your fashionista friends to miniature edible versions of your favourite It Bag.

Makes 20 pops

Ingredients
20 medium cake balls, chilled
100g (¼ bag) each white, pink and lavender candy melts
100g (¼ bag) black or brown candy melts
80g black or brown sugarpaste, kneaded

Equipment
Disposable piping bag

Make handles in advance: roll the sugarpaste into a log shape with your hands. With a small knife, cut into 20 strips, making some 4cm long and others 2cm long, then form each piece into a 'U' shape. Leave on baking paper to dry overnight.

Shape each cake ball into a rectangle with slanted sides. Try making some rectangles longer or wider than others for variety.

Melt each colour of candy melts separately. Working with 5 pops per colour, dip the end of each lollipop stick 2cm deep into the candy and insert a stick through the bottom of each pop. Leave to set. Dip each pop fully into its respective colour of candy and shake off any excess. Insert into a polystyrene block to dry.

Quickly pour the remaining black or brown candy into the piping bag. Cut a small piece off the tip and pipe details such as seams, clasps and logos on the bags. Use the candy in the piping bag to attach the handles to each bag. Place the pops back in the polystyrene block to set.

ICE CREAM CONE POPS

Perfect for a picnic on a sunny day. Add a fun and realistic touch with drips of candy and colourful sprinkles.

Makes 10 pops

Ingredients
10 small cake balls
10 medium cake balls
200g (½ bag) each light brown and white candy melts
200g (½ bag) pink, yellow or lavender candy melts
Sprinkles

Roll each medium cake ball between your palms into a cone shape. Repeat with the rest of the medium balls.

Push one side of each small cake ball onto a flat surface to flatten it slightly. Repeat with the rest of the small balls.

To assemble the ice cream pops: melt and mix together all of the light brown candy and ¾ white candy to make a caramel colour. Dip the end of each lollipop stick 2cm into the candy. Insert halfway into the thinner end of the cone. Now dip the surface of the top end of the cone into the candy and stick the flat side of a small cake ball onto it. Repeat with each pop and once the candy has set dip the entire thing into the bowl. Insert into a polystyrene block to dry.

Now melt seperately the pink, yellow and lavender candy and dip the top third of the cake pop, just to where the small ball meets the cone, into your chosen colour. If you're feeling adventurous, holding the pop vertically, tap the bottom of the stick onto your kitchen surface. This will create fantastically authentic-looking ice cream drips.

Melt the rest of the white candy melts with an extra drop of vegetable oil. Using a teaspoon drizzle over the top of the ice cream pop. Give it a little shake to create drips. Sprinkle with hundreds and thousands.

To finish off: take a cocktail stick and softly score diagonal lines across the cone to give a diamond pattern.

DONUT POPS

Double the sweetness, and who can say no to a donut? Combine the two for a totally poptastic treat.

Makes 20 pops

Ingredients
20 medium cake balls, chilled
400g (1 bag) light brown candy melts
200g (½ bag) white candy melts
Edible sprinkles, to decorate

Equipment
Medium ball tool

Take the cake balls and flatten them to form a donut shape. Next take the ball tool and gently push it into the centre of the donut to make a dent. Make sure you make enough of a dent for it to show through when the pop has been dipped in the candy. Chill for 10 minutes.

Melt and mix together the brown candy melts and three-quarters of the white candy melts to create a caramel colour.

Dip the end of each lollipop stick 2cm deep into the melted candy and insert a stick through the side of each donut about halfway in. Leave to set. Dip the donut pops in the candy and tap off the excess into the bowl. Place in a polystyrene block to dry.

In a separate bowl, melt the rest of the white candy. It's important that this is runnier than usual so add an extra drop of vegetable oil. Now take the teaspoon and drizzle the candy around the dent of the donuts. Shake on the sprinkles as you go. Place the pops back in the polystyrene block to dry.

TEA PARTY POPS

Afternoon tea has never been more popular. What could be a more fitting companion than your very own tea party set of cake pops?

Makes 10 teapots and 10 cups and saucers

Ingredients
20 medium cake balls, chilled
400g (1 bag) white candy melts
100g sugarpaste, kneaded and tinted pink
Edible glue
1 bottle white cocoa butter
1 tube edible dusting powder

Equipment
Rolling pin
3.8cm round fondant cutter
2 paintbrushes (1 thin, 1 medium)
Artist's palette

Make in advance
Saucers: roll out half the sugarpaste to 4mm thick and cut out 20 circles with the fondant cutter. Using the end of a lollipop stick, poke holes the same size as the sticks into the middle of the circles.

Handles: roll out a long, thin log shape of half the remaining sugarpaste. Cut out 10 x 4cm-long pieces for the teapot handles and 10 x 3cm-long pieces for the teacup handles. Form each handle into a 'C' shape.

Domed lids and knobs: using the remaining sugarpaste, roll 10 x 2.5cm-diameter balls of sugarpaste with your hands. Cut off the top third and bottom third of each ball – this will give you 20 domes for the lids. Roll 20 x 5mm-diameter balls for the knobs, using your hands, and glue to the top centre of each dome, dabbing on the edible glue with the thin paintbrush.

For the teapots

Take 10 of the chilled cake balls and separate a small (2g) piece of mixture from each ball. Re-roll the larger balls and squash the bottom of each ball down flat. For the teapot spouts, take the 10 x 2g pieces of cake pop mixture and roll each piece into a log shape with your thumb and forefinger. Shape it so that one end of the log is thinner than the other. Set aside in the fridge.

For the teacups

Take the remaining 10 chilled cake balls and place on a flat surface, pushing the bottom of each ball down on the surface. You want the top of the cups to be completely flat, so push down and smooth the sides down until you get a half-ball shape. Set aside in the fridge.

Melt the white candy melts. Remove the teacup and teapot shapes from the fridge. Using a cocktail stick, dab a little candy on the thicker end of the spouts and attach them to the teapots. Make sure they are facing the right way up.

Dip the end of each lollipop stick 2cm deep into the candy. Insert a stick into the flatter end of each teapot and into the round end of each teacup.

Dip each teapot fully into the candy. Be extra gentle so that the spout doesn't fall off. Attach the lids to the teapots before the candy sets.

Next, dip each teacup into the candy and attach the saucers to the bottom of the teacups by sliding them up the sticks.

Insert each cake pop into a polystyrene block to dry – 1–2 minutes per pop.

Once the cake pops have dried, attach the handles by using a small dab of candy on a cocktail stick to secure them.

Melt the cocoa butter and tint 1 teaspoonful with the dusting powder. Use the thicker paintbrush to paint beautiful vintage-style patterns on the teapots with the cocoa butter. Keep it simple – dots, swirls, stripes all look really cute.

SLICE OF CAKE

It might be stating the obvious but I love cake, so it's only right that a slice gets featured in this book! Choose any flavour of cake you like for these pops – vanilla, chocolate, red velvet, toffee, lemon or even peanut butter.

Makes 20 pops

Ingredients
20 medium cake balls, chilled
200g (½ bag) each white and brown candy melts
20 red Smarties
Mulit-coloured edible sprinkles
50g pink or red candy melts

Equipment
2 disposable piping bags

Shape each cake ball into a wedge with the shorter side of the wedge slightly rounded.

Melt the white and brown candy separately. Dip 10 lollipop sticks 2cm into the brown candy and the other 10 sticks 2cm into the white candy and insert a stick into the centre of each wedge. Leave to set. Now dip each pop fully into the candy, dipping 10 pops into the brown and 10 into the white, and shake off the excess. Insert into a polystyrene block to dry.

Dip the top 1cm of each white cake pop into the brown candy, then dip the top 1cm of the rounded edge into the candy. Place a Smartie on top of each pop and decorate with sprinkles as you go. Do the same with the brown cake pops but dip them into the white candy. Place back in the polystyrene block to dry. Melt the pink or red candy. Pour into the piping bag and cut a small piece off the tip. Pipe a pink or red horizontal line across the sides of each cake pop. Do the same with the remaining white candy. Place back in the polystyrene block to set.

SUSHI

These sushi-inspired cake balls look so realistic you could serve them as canapés at your next party and astonish all your guests.

Makes 20

Ingredients
20 medium cake balls, chilled
400g (1 bag) white candy melts
100g (¼ bag) each orange and red candy melts
White sugar strands or jimmies
50g black sugarpaste, kneaded

Equipment
Rolling pin
Small palette knife

Split each cake ball in half. Keeping them in pairs, shape each half into a rectangular block – they can be irregular sizes.

Melt the white candy. Stick each pair of blocks together, using the candy as glue, and insert a cocktail stick into each sushi piece. Leave to set. Place a sheet of baking paper under a wire rack. Holding it by the cocktail stick, dip each piece fully into the white candy and shake off the excess. Run the cocktail stick through the wire rack and leave to set.

Melt the orange and red candy separately. Dip the top half of 10 sushi pieces into the red candy and the other 10 into the orange candy. While the orange candy is still wet, use a cocktail stick to draw chevrons on it with the white candy. Give it a gentle shake to smooth it out. Return to the wire rack to dry.

Dab the remaining white candy around the bottom of each piece, sprinkling the white sugar strands as you go. Remove the cocktail sticks and leave to set.

Roll out the black sugarpaste and cut out 20 strips about 1.5cm wide and 10cm long. Working quickly before the sugarpaste dries, wrap them around the side of each piece. Place on a tray lined with baking paper to set.

FLOWERPOTS

Ideal for Mother's Day, these beautiful flowerpots are a more inspired choice than the traditional bouquet. You can make the roses yourself or buy ready-made ones.

Makes 20 pops

Ingredients
20 medium cake balls
200g (½ bag) each orange and
   red candy melts
50g green candy melts
25g each of white and pink
   (or yellow and lavender)
   sugarpaste, kneaded

Equipment
Rolling pin
Small palette knife
Disposable piping bag

Make roses in advance: roll out the 2 colours of sugarpaste to 2mm thick. With a palette knife, cut out 40 strips of each colour, about 2cm wide and 10cm long. Using your fingers, roll each strip into simple rose shapes. You will need 4 roses per cake pop.

For each cake ball, break off a 10g piece and set aside. Roll the rest of the ball into a log shape. Make one end of the 'log' thinner than the other end to form the bottom of the flowerpot.

   Take the small piece of cake ball, reroll it and flatten into a 6mm-thick circle so that it is slightly bigger than the top of the flowerpot.

   Melt the orange and red candy melts together. Dip the top of each flowerpot into the candy and stick the flat circles on top. Leave to set. Dip the end of each lollipop stick 2cm deep into the candy and insert a stick into the bottom of each pop. Leave to set. Then dip each pop fully into the candy and insert into a polystyrene block to dry.

   Using a dab of candy on a cocktail stick as glue, arrange the roses on top of the flowerpot and secure in place.

   Melt the green candy. Quickly pour into the piping bag, cut a small piece off the tip and pipe leaves around the roses. Place the pops back in the polystyrene block to set.

SHEEP

Create your own pop farm with these sheep. They require a little more patience than the other designs, so set aside some extra time.

Makes 20

Ingredients
20 medium cake balls, chilled
400g (1 bag) white candy melts
200g (½ bag) black candy melts
20 small edible heart sprinkles
40 small M&M's
1 bottle cocoa butter
1 tube each pink and black edible
  dusting powder

Equipment
Thin paintbrush
Artist's palette

Break a 5g piece from each cake ball and roll it for the head. Melt the white candy. Insert a cocktail stick into each larger cake ball, then dip fully into the candy and shake off any excess. Run the cocktail sticks through a wire rack placed over a sheet of baking paper and leave to set.

Dip each larger cake ball once more into the candy, using a cocktail stick to texturise the candy before it sets. Build up layers of curls.

Melt the black candy. Stick a heart sprinkle, pointed side up, on either side of each small ball to form the ears. Dip the back of each ball into the black candy and attach it to each white-coated cake ball. One by one, hold each pop by its cocktail stick and carefully dip the 'head' into the black candy, making sure the ears are coated too. Shake off any excess, then run the sticks through the wire rack and leave to set.

For the legs, use candy to attach 4 candy-dipped M&M's to the bottom of each pop. Melt the cocoa butter. In the palette, tint 1 teaspoonful each with the 2 dusting powders and leave a third white. On each sheep, paint 2 white dots with a smaller black dot in the middle for the eyes. Use pink to paint the noses.

Remove the cocktail sticks, place the sheep on a tray lined with baking paper and leave in the fridge until the cocoa butter has set.

CHICKENS

Cluck cluck, what's a farm without chickens? Use heart sprinkles to make beaks and combs to ensure your chickens look super-cute.

Makes 20

Ingredients
20 medium cake balls, chilled
200g (½ bag) each white and brown candy melts
80 edible heart sprinkles
1 bottle cocoa butter
1 tube black edible dusting powder

Equipment
Thin paintbrush
Artist's palette

Form each cake ball into an oblong shape, then elongate one end upwards into a bulb shape for the chicken's head. Shape the other end into a point for the tail.

   Melt the white and brown candy separately. Insert a cocktail stick into each chicken, then dip 10 of them into the white candy and the other 10 into the brown. Shake off the excess. While the candy is still wet, attach 3 hearts to the top of each head for the comb, then run the cocktail sticks through a wire rack placed over a sheet of baking paper and leave to set.

   For each chicken, use a dab of candy on a cocktail stick to attach the curved end of 2 heart sprinkles to the front of the head to form the beak.

   Melt the cocoa butter. In the palette, tint 1 teaspoonful with the dusting powder and leave 1 teaspoonful white. One by one, take hold of each chicken by its cocktail stick, paint a white dot for the eyes, then paint a smaller black dot inside each white dot. Use the black colour to paint details such as feathers. Remove the sticks, then put them on a tray lined with baking paper and place in the fridge until the cocoa butter has set.

GIRAFFES

My favourite animal just had to be turned into a cake pop. Giraffes are such attractive creatures – don't forget to give them big eyes with long lashes!

Makes 20 pops

Ingredients
20 medium cake balls, chilled
200g (½ bag) each orange and yellow candy melts
40 tic tacs
1 bottle white cocoa butter
1 tube each brown and black edible dusting powder

Equipment
Fine paintbrush
Artist's palette

Roll each cake ball into an oblong shape, making one end slightly narrower than the other.
  Melt the 2 colours of candy together. Using a cocktail stick, dab a little candy on each tic tac and attach 2 to the top of each pop to represent the horns. Leave to dry.
  Dip the end of each lollipop stick 2cm deep into the candy. Insert a stick into the bottom of each pop, pushing it through the centre of the wider end. Leave to set. Dip each pop fully into the candy and shake off any excess. Insert into a polystyrene block to dry.
  Melt the cocoa butter. In the palette tint 1 teaspoonful each with the 2 dusting powders and leave 1 teaspoonful white. Paint large dots for the eyes with the white colour. Use the black colour to paint smaller dots into the eyes and then to paint the eyelashes and nostrils. With the brown colour paint irregular patches on the giraffe. Place the pops back in the polystyrene block and leave in the fridge until the cocoa butter has set.

MONKEYS

These cheeky looking monkeys are such fun and their simple features make them quick and easy to put together.

Makes 20 pops

Ingredients
20 medium cake balls, chilled
400g (1 bag) light brown candy melts
50g caramel candy melts (or mix 1/3 brown with 2/3 white)
60 chocolate buttons
1 bottle cocoa butter
1 tube black edible dusting powder

Equipment
Thin paintbrush
Artist's palette

Flatten each cake ball slightly. Melt the light brown candy. Using a cocktail stick, dab a little candy on 40 of the chocolate buttons and attach 1 button to either side of each cake ball for the monkey's ears.

Dip the end of each lollipop stick 2cm deep into the candy and insert a stick through bottom of each cake ball. Leave to set. Dip each pop fully into the candy and shake off any excess. Using the remaining chocolate buttons, attach one to the front of each pop and secure in position. Insert into a polystyrene block to dry.

Melt the caramel candy. Scoop up 1 tablespoonful and carefully dip the chocolate button on the front of each pop into the candy. Next, use the candy to paint the inside of the ears and then to paint a heart shape on the top half of the face. Place in the polystyrene block to dry.

Melt the cocoa butter. In the palette tint 1 teaspoonful with the dusting powder and leave 1 teaspoonful white. Use the white colour to paint the eyes. Finally, use the black colour to paint black dots on each eye and to paint the nose and mouth on each pop. Place back in the polystyrene block and leave in the fridge for 10 minutes until the cocoa butter has set.

POKER CHIPS

Become a croupier for the night and host your own Vegas party with these easy poker chip pops.

Makes 20 pops

Ingredients
20 medium cake balls, chilled
400g (1 bag) white candy melts
1 bottle white cocoa butter
1 tube each red, blue and green edible dusting powder

Equipment
5cm round biscuit or pastry cutter
Paintbrush
Artist's palette

Flatten the cake balls and shape each one into a 2cm-thick circle by pushing it into the biscuit or pastry cutter. Remove and then smooth the edges with moistened fingers. Place in the fridge for 10 minutes to harden.

Melt the white candy. Dip the end of each lollipop stick 2cm deep into the candy and insert into the edge of each cake pop. Leave to set. Now dip each cake pop fully into the candy and shake off the excess. Insert into a polystyrene block to dry.

Melt the cocoa butter and tint 1 teaspoonful each with the 3 dusting powders. Paint a circle around the edge of each pop, leaving a 1cm border. Now paint squares all the way round in the border, leaving a gap between each one. Finally, paint the poker numbers in the centre of each pop. Insert into the polystyrene block and leave in the fridge until the cocoa butter has set.

POKER DICE

Roll your own dice! You can bet these simple but graphic pops will go down well with the boys.

Makes 20 pops

Ingredients
20 medium cake balls, chilled
200g (½ bag) each white and black candy melts
1 bottle white cocoa butter
1 tube black edible dusting powder

Equipment
Thin paintbrush
Artist's palette

Shape each cake ball into a cube with your hands, flattening the sides by pushing them down on a flat surface.

Melt the 2 colours of candy separately. Working with 10 cake pops per colour, dip the end of each lollipop stick 2cm deep into the candy and insert a stick into each pop. Leave to set. Dip each cake pop fully into its respective colour of candy and shake off the excess. Insert into a polystyrene block to dry.

Melt the cocoa butter. In the palette, tint 1 teaspoonful with the dusting powder and leave 1 teaspoonful white. Paint white dots on the black cubes and black dots on the white cubes in the same sequences as dice: opposite sides should add up to 7 – that is, 6 dots opposite 1, 5 opposite 2 and 4 opposite 3. Insert into the polystyrene block and leave in the fridge until the cocoa butter has set.

WEDDING ROSE POPS

Minimal and pretty – a modern twist on the traditional wedding cake. The rose design is a favourite with my customers. Try making these with the classic Vanilla Sponge recipe on page 22.

Makes 20 pops

Ingredients
20 medium cake balls, chilled
400g (1 bag) white candy melts
Edible white sprinkles, to decorate
50g white sugarpaste, kneaded

Equipment
Medium rose mould (see page 146 for stockists)

Make roses in advance: break the sugarpaste into 20 pieces and, one by one, push each piece into the mould, cutting off any excess with a small knife. Remove from the mould and place on a sheet of baking paper. Leave to dry overnight.

Melt the white candy. Dip the end of each lollipop stick 2cm deep into the candy and insert a stick into each cake ball. Leave to set.

   Dip each cake pop fully into the candy and decorate each one by attaching a rose to the top while still wet. Decorate with white sprinkles and insert into a polystyrene block to dry.

RATTLE POPS

Simple and cute, these are perfect for baby showers. Whether it's a girl or a boy, keep it sweet with sugar pearls or sprinkles.

Makes 20 pops

Ingredients
20 medium cake balls, chilled
400g (1 bag) candy melts in base colour of your choice
100g (¼ bag) candy melts in blue or pink
Sugar confetti, mini edible heart sprinkles or sugar pearls

Melt the base colour of candy. Dip the end of each lollipop stick 2cm deep into the candy and insert a stick into each cake ball. Leave to set. Then dip each cake ball fully into the base colour of candy and shake off the excess. Insert into a polystyrene block to dry.

Melt the blue or pink candy. Dip each cake pop halfway into the candy. Make sure you dip straight down to create even lines. Gently tap the excess into the bowl. Insert into the polystyrene block to dry.

Use the remaining candy to glue sugar confetti or other edible sprinkles or sugar pearls in a horizontal line around the centre of each pop.

TEDDIES

More adventurous than some of the other designs but surprisingly simple to make. They are a lovely way to welcome a new baby.

Makes 10 pops

Ingredients
10 medium cake balls, chilled
10 small cake balls, chilled
400g (1 bag) white candy melts
20g pink or blue candy melts
10 chocolate buttons, each cut in half
10 Smarties
40 chocolate M&M's
1 bottle white cocoa butter
1 tube black edible dusting powder

Equipment
2 paintbrushes (1 thin, 1 medium)
Artist's palette

Take a medium cake ball and flatten it slightly to form an oblong shape for his body. Pinch one end to make him slightly thinner on top. Melt the white candy. Use it to glue a small cake ball on top for the head and leave to set.

Now attach the other body parts, glueing them in place with candy. Use 2 chocolate button halves for the ears, placing one on either side of the head near the top. Attach a Smartie in the centre of the head for the nose. Use the M&M's for the arms and legs. Repeat with the remaining pops.

Dip the end of each lollipop stick 2.5cm deep into the candy and insert a stick through the bottom of each teddy. Chill for 20 minutes, or until firm.

Gently dip the front of each cake pop into the candy first and immediately turn it to dip the back. Carefully shake off the excess candy, then insert into a polystyrene block to dry.

Melt the pink or blue candy. Scoop into a teaspoon and dip the arms, legs and ears of each teddy into the candy. Place back in the polystyrene block to dry.

Melt the cocoa butter and tint 1 teaspoonful black with the dusting powder. Paint the nose, eyes and mouth on each teddy. Place in the fridge until the cocoa butter has set.

ALPHABET BLOCKS

These classic toy pops will transport you right back to childhood. They're perfect for celebrating those early years.

Makes 20 pops

Ingredients
20 cake balls, chilled
400g (1 bag) yellow candy melts
100g (¼ bag) candy melts in blue, green or red

Equipment
Disposable piping bag

Shape each cake ball into a square block, pushing each one against a flat surface to flatten the sides.

Melt the yellow candy. Dip the end of each lollipop stick 2cm deep into the candy and insert a stick into each cake ball. Leave to set. Then dip each ball fully into the candy and shake off the excess. Insert into a polystyrene block to dry.

Melt the secondary colour of candy, then quickly pour it into the piping bag before the candy sets. Cut a small piece off the tip of the bag. Pipe straight lines of candy all around the edges of the pops. Insert into the polystyrene block to set. Now pipe letters of your choice on each side of the pops. Place back in the polystyrene block to dry.

Tip: if the candy sets before you finish, just place the piping bag in a bowl in the microwave for 10 seconds at a time until it reaches the right consistency.

CLOWNS

Surely the most fun you can have with a cake pop? These are bright, colourful and not at all scary. You can choose just one colour for the hats or make them in different colours.

Makes 20 pops

Ingredients
20 medium cake balls, chilled
400g (1 bag) white candy melts
20g each green, blue and red candy melts
100g sugarpaste in different colours of your choice, kneaded
40g red sugarpaste, kneaded
1 bottle coloured confetti sprinkles
Edible glue
1 bottle white cocoa butter
1 tube each red and black edible dusting powder

Equipment
2 paintbrushes (1 thin, 1 medium)
Artist's palette

Make in advance
Hats: break the 100g sugarpaste into 20 x 5g pieces and form each one into a hat or cone shape. Using a little edible glue on a paintbrush, secure the confetti sprinkles in place on the shapes. Leave to dry overnight on baking paper.
Noses: break the red sugarpaste into 20 equal pieces and roll into balls. Leave to dry overnight on baking paper.

Melt the white candy. Dip the end of each lollipop stick 2cm deep into the candy and insert a stick into each cake ball. Leave to set. Now dip each ball fully in the candy and gently tap off the excess. Place a hat on top of each ball while the candy is still wet. Insert into a polystyrene block to dry. Next, attach the noses to the faces as you go, glueing them in place with a dab of candy. Leave to dry.

Melt the additional candy colours separately. Using a cocktail stick, paint the hair onto each cake pop. Be as creative as you like. The first layer will be very thin, so leave each one to dry before adding another. Gradually build up more layers of hair and use the cocktail sticks to texturise them. You may need to do this up to 5 times per cake pop. Leave to set.

Next, paint the eyebrows diagonally across the top third of each clown's face, using a dab of candy on a cocktail stick. Try using contrasting colours for the eyebrows and the hair.

Melt the cocoa butter and tint 1 teaspoonful each with the 2 dusting powders. Paint on a big smiling mouth with the red candy. Paint big black dots for the eyes, then paint lines in the shape of a cross around them. Finally, paint a black line in the middle of the red mouth in the shape of a smile. Place the pops back in the polystyrene block and leave in the fridge for 10 minutes to allow the cocoa butter to set.

BIG TOP

The simplest things can look so beautiful. The iconic big top tent gets a pop makeover. Just shape it, dip it, paint the stripes and you've got your very own circus.

Makes 20 pops

Ingredients
20 medium cake balls, chilled
400g (1 bag) white candy melts
10g blue sugarpaste, kneaded
1 bottle white cocoa butter
1 tube each red and black
   edible dusting powder

Equipment
Rolling pin
Thin paintbrush
Artist's palette

Make flags in advance: roll out all of the sugarpaste to 2mm thick. Using a small knife cut out 20 small triangles about 1cm wide and 50mm deep. Leave to dry overnight on baking paper.

Break one-third off each cake ball. Keep the 2 pieces in pairs. For each pair, use your hands to shape the larger piece into a chunky cylinder. Shape the smaller piece into a wide cone that fits perfectly on top of the cylinder. Melt the candy and use to stick the 2 pieces together.

   Dip the end of each lollipop stick 2cm deep into the candy and insert a stick into each pop. Leave to set. Now dip each pop fully into the candy, then stick a flag on top of each pop and insert into a polystyrene block to dry.

   To decorate: melt the cocoa butter and tint 1 teaspoonful each with the 2 dusting powders. Paint stripes on the pops with the red colour and then paint a door with the black colour. Insert into the polystyrene block to dry and place in the fridge for 10 minutes to allow the cocoa butter to set.

SNOWMEN

Were snowmen invented just so they could be turned into cake pops? I think so!
The simple sugarpaste hats, noses and scarves make them look really authentic.

Makes 10 pops

Ingredients
10 small cake balls, chilled
10 medium cake balls, chilled
400g (1 bag) white candy melts
70g black sugarpaste, kneaded
10g orange sugarpaste, kneaded
Edible glue
50g light blue or red sugarpaste, kneaded
1 bottle white cocoa butter
1 tube black edible dusting powder

Equipment
Thin paintbrush
Artist's palette

Make in advance
Hats: roll just under half the black sugarpaste into 10 x 3g balls, then push down
on each one with your thumb to form flat discs for the rims of the hats. Roll the
remaining black sugarpaste into 10 x 4g balls and shape each ball into a tube
that has a flat top and bottom. Using the paintbrush, dab a little edible glue
on the bottom of each tube, then place each one on a flat disc and leave to
set overnight.
Noses: roll the orange sugarpaste into 10 balls. Mould them into carrot shapes
by rolling them between your fingers and making one end thinner than the other.
Leave on baking paper to set overnight.

Melt the white candy. Dip the bottom of each small cake ball into the candy, then
stick on top of a medium cake ball.

Dip the end of each lollipop stick 2cm deep into the candy and insert a stick into each snowman. Leave to set. (If the cake balls have softened, place them back in the fridge for 10 minutes.) Dip each pop fully into the white candy and then place a hat on each snowman as you go. Insert into a polystyrene block to dry.

Once the pops have dried, use a cocktail stick to glue the carrots into the middle of each snowman's face with the remaining white candy.

For the eyes, mouth and buttons: melt the cocoa butter and tint 1 teaspoonful black with the dusting powder. Paint black eyes, mouths and buttons on the snowmen. Insert the pops into the polystyrene block and place in the fridge for about 10 minutes until the cocoa butter has set.

For the scarves: roll out the blue or red sugarpaste, then cut into long, thin strips about 10cm long and 1.5cm wide. Working quickly before the sugarpaste dries, attach the scarves to the snowmen by draping them in place. The sugarpaste will glue itself into place as it dries.

CHRISTMAS PUDDINGS

Love or loathe Christmas pudding, no one will say no to these. For a really festive touch make them with Red Velvet Cake or Chocolate Cake (see recipes on pages 26 and 25)

Makes 20

Ingredients
20 cake balls, chilled
400g (1 bag) dark brown candy melts
100g (¼ bag) white candy melts
Small holly icing decorations

Place a sheet of baking paper under a wire rack.

Melt the dark brown candy. Insert a cocktail stick into each cake ball. Dip each fully into the candy, gently shake off any excess and run the cocktail sticks through the wire rack to dry as you go.

Melt the white candy, adding an extra drop of vegetable oil to make it extra-runny. Using a teaspoon, spoon the candy over the top of each cake and give it a little shake. The candy should start dripping down the sides – if you'd like it to drip more, hold the cake by its cocktail stick and tap it vertically on a flat surface a couple of times.

While the white candy is still wet, decorate the cakes with the holly icing, then remove the cocktail sticks and place on a tray lined with baking paper to dry.

VALENTINE'S HEARTS

Nothing spells 'Love' more than a classic heart shape. Try making these with Red Velvet Cake balls (see cake and frosting recipes on pages 26 and 22) for an extra romantic touch.

Makes 20 pops

Ingredients
20 medium cake balls, chilled
200g (½ bag) each red and pink candy melts
Edible sprinkles, to decorate

Flatten each cake ball and, using your hands, shape the bottom end of each ball into a 'V'. Using a lollipop stick, make an indentation in the top of the 'V' and then curve the top left and top right sides to form a heart shape. Set aside in the fridge to chill.

   Melt the red and pink candy separately. Dip each lollipop stick 2cm deep into the candy, dipping 10 sticks in the red candy and the remainder in the pink. Insert a stick about halfway into each heart through the bottom end. Leave to set.

   Now dip each heart fully into the candy, dipping 10 hearts in the red candy and the remainder in the pink. Decorate with sprinkles as you go. Insert into a polystyrene block to dry.

EASTER EGG POPS

Bring these easy Easter eggs to life by piping different-coloured patterns on them. Be as creative as you like.

Makes 20 pops

Ingredients
20 medium cake balls, chilled
100g (¼ bag) each pink, blue, green and yellow candy melts
Selection of coloured confetti sprinkles, to decorate

Equipment
4 disposable piping bags

Start by rolling each cake ball into an oblong shape with your hands. Make the top narrower than the bottom so it resembles an egg shape.

Melt the different colours of candy separately. Working with 5 pops per colour, dip the end of each lollipop stick 2cm deep into the candy and insert a stick into the bottom of each egg. Leave to set. Dip each fully into its respective colour of candy and shake off the excess. Insert into a polystyrene block to dry.

Pour the remainder of the candy colours into 4 separate piping bags. Cut a small piece off each tip, then pipe patterns onto the eggs. Using a cocktail stick, dab a little candy on each sprinkle and glue into position on the eggs. Place back in the polystyrene block to dry.

BUNNIES

These adorable Easter bunnies are one of my favourite designs. I like to make them with the Lemon Cake (see recipe on page30).

Makes 20 pops

Ingredients
20 medium cake balls, chilled
400g (1 bag) white candy melts
120g white sugarpaste, kneaded
40 small M&M's
20 white mimosa ball sprinkles
40 small edible heart sprinkles
20 edible metallic dragee balls
1 bottle white cocoa butter
1 tube each black and pastel pink
 edible dusting powder

Equipment
Thin paintbrush
Artist's palette

Make ears in advance: separate the white sugarpaste into 40 pieces. For each ear, roll a piece of sugarpaste into a teardrop shape. Elongate one end until you have a long bunny ear. Leave to dry overnight on baking paper.

Shape each cake ball into an oval. Melt the candy. Using a dab of candy, glue a pair of ears to the top of each cake ball. Attach 2 M&M's at the bottom for the legs.
 Dip the end of each lollipop stick 2cm deep into the candy and insert a stick through the bottom of each cake pop. Leave to set. Dip each cake pop fully into the candy and shake off the excess. Stick a mimosa ball sprinkle on the back of each for the tail. Insert into a polystyrene block to dry.
 To attach the bows, use the remaining white candy melts and a cocktail stick to glue 2 heart sprinkles in place at the top of each bunny's head and place a metallic dragee in the centre.
 Melt the cocoa butter and tint 1 teaspoonful each with the 2 dusting powders. Use the pink colour to paint the bunny's nose and to fill in the inside of the ears. Use the black colour to paint the eyes. Insert into the polystyrene block and place in the fridge for 10 minutes until the cocoa butter has set.

HALLOWEEN PUMPKINS

I love Halloween as it means I get to carve a pumpkin. Make these pumpkin pops in seasonal toffee flavour (see the Toffee Cake recipe on page 29).

Makes 20 pops

Ingredients
20 medium cake balls, chilled
400g (1 bag) orange candy melts
20g green candy melts
1 bottle white cocoa butter
1 tube black edible dusting powder

Equipment
Thin paintbrush
Artist's palette
Disposable piping bag

Melt the orange candy. Dip the end of each lollipop stick 2cm deep into the candy and insert a stick into each cake ball. Leave to set. Dip each cake ball fully into the candy and shake off the excess. Place on a sheet of baking paper with the sticks facing up. Leave to set.

Melt the green candy, then pour into the piping bag and cut a small piece off the tip of the bag. Pipe a green stalk on each cake pop around the stick. Leave to set.

Melt the cocoa butter and tint 1 teaspoonful black with the dusting powder. With the paintbrush, paint black triangles for the eyes and nose, then paint a thick zig-zag line for the mouth.

Place the pops back on the baking paper and leave in the fridge for 10 minutes until the cocoa butter has set.

HORROR SHOW

ZOMBIE HEADS

I originally made these for the opening of Eat Your Heart Out, the world's first over-18s cake shop in Shoreditch, East London, where there were hour-long queues for gory cakes. This zombie head design is one of the most fun pops to make.

Makes 20 pops

Ingredients
20 medium cake balls, chilled
400g (1 bag) spooky green candy melts
20g pink candy melts
50g red candy melts
40g white sugarpaste, kneaded
1 black and 1 green edible ink pen

Equipment
Disposable piping bag

Make eyes in advance: roll the sugarpaste into 40 small balls. Leave to harden overnight.

Paint the eyes on the sugarpaste, using the black pen for the pupil and the green pen for the iris.

Shape the cake balls into irregular ovals for the zombie heads. Melt the green candy. Dip the end of each lollipop stick 2cm deep in the candy and insert a stick into each cake ball. Leave to set. Dip each cake ball fully into the green candy and shake off the excess. While the candy is still wet, attach an eye on the left side of each face. Insert into a polystyrene block to dry.

Using a cocktail stick, dab the green candy around the left eye on each head.

For the brain, melt the pink candy, then dip the very top of each head into the pink candy and leave to set.

For the blood, melt the red candy, quickly pour into a piping bag and cut a small piece off the tip of the bag. For each pop, pipe the eye socket for the right eye in red and place the remaining eyeball over it. Pipe a trail of blood coming out of the eye with the red candy. Now pipe red blood around the pink brain and then pipe drips of blood pouring down the face. Pipe red candy around the stick, then turn the cake pop upside down and give it a little shake. Insert into the polystyrene block to dry.

Using a cocktail stick, score the pattern of the brain on the top of each pop. Using your finger, dab a little red candy over it and blend it in. Place back in the polystyrene block and leave to set.

EYEBALLS

These eyeballs, complete with stalks, look so real. You'd be surprised how many people love to eat cake that looks like body parts. For extra gore make the cake balls with the Red Velvet Cake (see recipe on pages 26 and 22).

Makes 20 pops

Ingredients
20 medium cake balls, chilled
400g (1 bag) white candy melts
20g red candy melts
1 bottle white cocoa butter
1 tube each black, green and
   red edible dusting powder

Equipment
Disposable piping bag
2 paintbrushes (1 thin,1 medium)
Artist's palette

Melt the white candy. Dip the end of each lollipop stick 2cm in the candy and insert a stick into each cake ball. Leave to set. Dip each cake ball fully into the candy and shake off the excess. Insert into a polystyrene block to dry.

Melt the red candy, pour into the piping bag and cut a small piece off the tip of the bag. Pipe the candy over the bottom of the cake pop around the stick to form the root of the eyeball. Leave to set.

Melt the cocoa butter and tint 1 teaspoonful each with the 3 dusting powders. Paint the top of each cake pop with the black colour to represent the pupil of the eyeball. Paint the iris around the pupil in green. Then paint red blood vessels around the eyes. Place in the polystyrene block and refrigerate for 10 minutes until the cocoa butter has set.

SKULLS

These pops were inspired by the Mexican Day of the Dead celebrations. Prettify the skulls by adding sprinkles and painting patterns on them. The Red Velvet Cake is a fitting choice of flavour for these (see recipe on pages 26 and 22).

Makes 20 pops

Ingredients
20 medium cake balls, chilled
400g (1 bag) white candy melts
1 bottle white cocoa butter
1 tube each black, red, green and yellow edible dusting powder
Sugar flower and heart sprinkles (optional)

Equipment
Medium ball tool
Thin paintbrush
Artist's palette

Roll each cake ball into an oblong with your hands, then mould into the shape of a skull. Squeeze the bottom half of the oblong inwards to shape the jaw. Using the ball tool or your index finger, make 2 indentations for the eye sockets.

Melt the white candy. Dip the end of each lollipop stick 2cm deep into the candy and insert a stick into the neck of each skull. Leave to set. Dip each pop fully into the candy and shake off the excess. Insert into a polystyrene block to dry.

Melt the cocoa butter and tint 1 teaspoonful each with the 4 dusting powders. Paint the eye sockets black and paint a black mouth on each pop. Paint other details such as flowers and patterns with the other colours. Place on a tray lined with baking paper and leave in the fridge until the cocoa butter has set.

When set, you can either leave the cake pops as they are or decorate with flower sprinkles, using the remaining white candy and a cocktail stick to glue them on.

TECHNIQUES

Over the last 18 months, through trial and quite a bit of error I perfected the art of making cake pops. Looking back I can't believe how much I have learnt.

In this section you will find all the tips and tricks you need to get the best results when making cake pops. Learn how to store the individual ingredients at any stage of the popping process, how to paint beautiful designs with cocoa butter and how to make the cutest sugarpaste decorations.

BASIC STORAGE INSTRUCTIONS

You can bake the cake sponge up to 3 days in advance of making cake pops. It's actually easier to mix the frosting with a cake that's not freshly baked the same day, as the crumbs can sometimes be too soft.

If you're able to plan in advance, bake the cake sponge and let it cool. When cool, cover with clingfilm and store in an airtight container, but don't refrigerate.

You can make the frosting 2 days in advance but make sure you keep it in the fridge until it's needed. It's best to take it out and leave at room temperature about 2 hours before using.

Once you've combined the cake crumbs and frosting, wrap the mixture in clingfilm and refrigerate. At this point you will need to keep it in the fridge for at least 1 hour before rolling the cake balls or shapes. If necessary, the cake pop mixture can be kept in the fridge for 3 days, as can rolled cake balls. Just keep them covered or in an airtight container.

The cake pop mixture and undipped balls can also be frozen for up to 3 months.

Once dipped, the cake pops can be refrigerated in a plastic airtight container for up to 1 week.

CAKE BALL SIZES

It's best to make standard sizes of cake balls so they all look the same as this makes it easier to decorate them.

You could weigh each ball on digital scales. A good weight is 30 grams. Or you could use a spoon to scoop the mixture and measure the size you want. As a guide, 1 tablespoon of cake pop mixture makes a small cake ball about 3cm in diameter, and 2 tablespoons makes a medium-sized, 3.8cm-diameter ball.

SHAPING CAKE BALLS

If you combine it properly, the mixture for cake pops is very versatile. You can mould it into all sorts of different shapes without it falling apart. This is great when it comes to making more elaborate designs. You can roll into long strips or taper it into cone shapes.

The ball tool is commonly used in cake decorating. I like to use it for detailing, such as the perfectly rounded indentations in the Donut Pops and the eyes in the Skull Pops. But if you don't have a ball tool you can just as well use your index finger.

GLUEING

For big glueing jobs, such as sticking two bits of cake ball together, it is best to use candy melts. You don't want your pops to fall apart and candy melts are surprisingly stubborn when they have dried. They will hold anything together!

For more detailed glueing work like sticking on sugarpaste decorations, use edible glue. With a paintbrush and edible glue you get a much finer finish so it is perfect for adding the finishing touches to designs that have already been painted.

OTHER USEFUL TOOLS FOR DECORATING

Paintbrushes: for painting pretty designs onto cake pops with cocoa butter or for piecing sugarpaste decorations together with edible glue.

Artist's palette: for mixing and colouring cocoa butter.

CREATING DIFFERENT COLOURS WITH CANDY MELTS

You can mix different colours of candy melts together to create new ones. If you need to lighten the colour, just add some white candy melts. Alternatively, you can use oil-based candy colours to tint white candy melts. To colour candy this way, start with a tiny drop of oil-based colour and stir. Keep adding a drop at a time until you reach the desired shade.

Note: Like chocolate, candy is oil-based, so do not mix it with water and don't use normal, non-oil-based food colourings with candy melts.

TIPS FOR MANAGING CANDY MELTS

Working out how much candy to use per project is tricky as it depends on your dipping skills, the size of the cake pops and what consistency you want to achieve. For a beginner, I would say that you will need a whole bag (400g) for 20 cake pops, half a bag (200g) for 10 cake pops, a quarter bag (100g) for 5 pops, and so on. Use this as a guide to work out how much candy to use when you want to mix different colours in each batch.

Most instructions say you can't reheat candy but I have successfully re-melted it. Just add a drop of vegetable oil before putting it into the microwave. When piping candy onto cake pops, should you find the candy sets before you finish, just place the piping bag in a bowl in the microwave for 10 seconds at a time until it reaches the right consistency.

If you have lots of candy left over after making cake pops, it's always worth trying to save it. Using a spatula, spread it over a sheet of baking paper and leave to set. Once it has set, break it up and store in a plastic food bag at room temperature.

MAKING SUGARPASTE DECORATIONS

Sugarpaste (also known as fondant) is the rolled icing often used to cover cakes. In this book it is used to make beautiful decorations to add to cake pops. Good-quality sugarpaste is widely available from cake craft shops or online (see page 146 for stockists).

You can make a whole variety of sugarpaste decorations to apply to cake pops by using tools such as biscuit or pastry cutters and silicone moulds. I have given instructions in the individual recipes for making the specific decorations for each cake pop design in this book, but use the directions below as a guide to preparing sugarpaste and to making decorations using silicone moulds.

Before you start to work with sugarpaste you must knead it to make it pliable. First you will need to add a powder called gum tragacanth or sugarcel – 1 teaspoon per 500 grams is required. This makes the sugarpaste strong and elastic. Using your hands, knead the powder into the sugarpaste to warm it up. Keep kneading for about 5 minutes until the sugarpaste stretches like chewing gum when you pull it apart.

To colour sugarpaste, simply dab a little food colouring (normal food colouring paste is fine) on the sugarpaste with a cocktail stick and knead until the colour is consistent and not streaky. Repeat until your desired shade is achieved.

You can stick individual parts of the sugarpaste decorations together with some edible glue applied with a paintbrush. To attach sugarpaste decorations to cake pops, use a dab of candy melts on a cocktail stick.

Sugarpaste can dry out easily so, when not in use, store in an airtight container. If you find it has dried out slightly, you can apply a little vegetable shortening such as Trex to sugarpaste before using.

MAKING SUGARPASTE DECORATIONS BY HAND

You'll want to make some sugarpaste designs for which there isn't a mould. The good news is sugarpaste is very easy to work with. It's like plasticine so you can shape it by hand, before painting and decorating it. So long as you knead it, it will be pliable and stretchy. You can flatten it into disks, squidge it into beads, and roll it into tubes. It'll shape itself into anything from teapot lids and handles to a snowman's scarf and earmuffs!

Make sure your hands are clean and free from water when handling sugarpaste, and it's best to wear light clothing too as it has a tendency to pick up stray fibres.

If you plan to make sugar decorations often it's useful to invest in a non-stick board.

USING SUGARPASTE WITH SILICONE MOULDS

Silicone moulds enable you to make a wide variety of different decorations to add character to cake pops. You can buy a huge range of moulds online (see page 146 for stockists). With diverse themes such as flowers, balloons, faces, sports, fashion, as well as seasonal moulds, you can find something for every occasion.

Try to judge how much sugarpaste will fit into each mould – you simply push it in, smooth your finger over it and pop it out seconds later. If you find you have used too little, just add more and smooth it out. If you have used too much, then cut off the excess with a knife. Leave to dry on baking paper.

Sugarpaste decorations should ideally be made in advance so they can dry fully

before you use them on cake pops – about 2 days in advance is perfect, but the day before is also fine. They can be stored in plastic airtight containers for several weeks.

For a beautiful shimmer effect, spray them with edible lustre or apply a little edible glue with a paintbrush and then sprinkle with edible glitter.

USING COCOA BUTTER FOR PAINTING

The easiest and most effective way to paint designs or patterns on cake pops is by using cocoa butter, which you melt first (see below) and then apply with a paintbrush. You can buy cocoa butter in bottles from specialist chocolate-making suppliers (see page 146 for stockists).

Cocoa butter comes in various colours but, when working with different colours, I like to use white cocoa butter and then tint it with edible dusting powder, which is food colouring in powder form. This is more cost-effective than buying different colours of cocoa butter. It is worth investing in a bottle as a little goes a long way.

To melt the cocoa butter, put the bottle into the microwave. Heat for 1 minute, shake the bottle well, heat for 1 minute more, then shake again. Once the cocoa butter has reached liquid consistency, pour 1 teaspoonful into an artist's palette. To colour it, sprinkle a little edible dusting powder into the cocoa butter and stir with a paintbrush. It's easy to tint cocoa butter in pastel colours but it can be tricky to get a true black or red. So keep adding a little more powder until you reach the desired shade. Colours can also be mixed together to create new shades. Repeat with as many colours as needed.

Any unused cocoa butter can be stored in the bottle at room temperature and the butter can be re-melted as many times as you like.

Cocoa butter is very fluid and easy to work with but has a tendency to dry out very quickly. The good news is that you can keep returning the artist's palette to the microwave for 10-second bursts. When you have finished painting, you can cover any leftover cocoa butter in the palette with clingfilm and reuse when needed. There's no need to refrigerate it.

Once you have painted the cake pops, you will need to put them on a tray lined with baking paper and place in the fridge for 10–15 minutes to allow the cocoa butter to set, otherwise your beautiful work will smudge.

USING EDIBLE INK PENS

These are excellent for drawing designs and patterns on sugarpaste. You can also use them instead of cocoa butter for drawing on cake pops, although they are not as fluid and tend to dry out quickly.

The pens come in a variety of colours and the best brand is Americolor (see page 146 for stockists).

PACKAGING AND PRESENTATION

Cake pops look even more beautiful when wrapped in little polythene bags. Just slip them into the bag and seal with a twist tie or a pretty ribbon.

They also make attractive gifts when presented in a chocolate box or small cake box. Line the box with coloured tissue paper first.

If you're making cake pops for a party and want to display them, try wrapping some polystyrene in printed paper or tissue paper and stick the pops in it. You could even make a tiered display with different-sized cake dummies. Vases filled with sprinkles also work well. Use the pages in this book as inspiration.

STOCKISTS

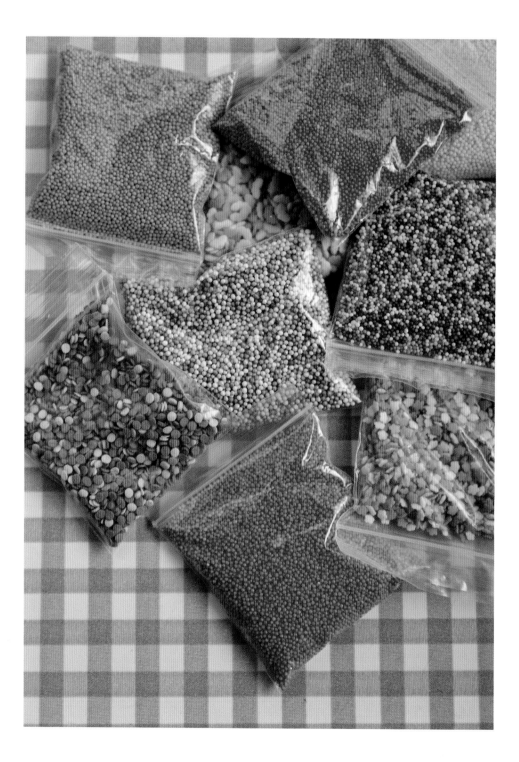

Cake pops and supplies such as lollipop sticks, twist ties, display stands and handmade decorations
www.mollybakes.co.uk

Cake decorating equipment and twist ties
www.cakecraftworld.co.uk

Cake making ingredients are available from most major supermarkets
www.allinsonflour.co.uk (nature friendly flour)
www.billingtons.co.uk (unrefined sugar)
www.greenandblacks.com (Fairtrade organic cocoa powder and chocolate)

Candy colouring, candy melts, edible ink pens and lollipop bags
www.thecakedecoratingcompany.co.uk
www.cakescookiesandcraftsshop.co.uk

Candy melts, lollipop sticks, sprinkles and sugarcraft equipment
www.cakescookiesandcraftsshop.co.uk
www.hobbycraft.co.uk
Sugarshack
Unit 12, Bowmans Trading Estate, Westmoreland Road, London NW9 9RL
   www.sugarshack.co.uk
Party Party
9-13 Ridley Road, Dalston, London E8 2NP
   www.ppshop.co.uk

Cocoa butter and edible dusting powder
www.homechocolatefactory.co.uk

Edible sprinkles, rose and violet petals, candy colouring oils and flavours
www.makeawishcakeshop.co.uk

Silicone moulds, including rose moulds and vintage button moulds
www.neitmoulds.co.uk

INDEX

ACKNOWLEDGEMENTS

Thanks to my mum who taught me how to bake, my dad for encouraging me to start selling my cakes, my sisters for all the hours of free help, and to my fiancé Olly for putting up with all the baking madness and putting the Olly into Molly.

To Rowan for giving me this fantastic opportunity and the rest of the wonderful team who have made this book so beautiful: Fred, Noel and Wei.
Special thanks to my two assistants Heather and Chloe. Thanks also to Cristian and Joe for their support.

Last but not least, thanks to Miss Cakehead for all the genius cake events she has organised, which inspired some of the edgier designs in this book.

'Molly Bakes', as she is known when baking, is surprisingly new to cakes. Two years ago, on the eve of her birthday, she found herself out of a job. Rather than mope, she took up baking for the very first time. She fell in love and has never looked back. Today her cake pops can be found everywhere from her Brick Lane stall to Selfridges, and include clients such as *Vogue* and fans like Eliza Doolittle.